Shades of Meaning

Marguerite Guzmán Bouvard

ACKNOWLEDGEMENTS

With thanks to the editors of the publications in which these poems appeared.

- Simone, Retreat, *Unlikely Stories.*
- Silence, Passage, This Strange Landscape, The Abbey of Sénanque, Pollen, Upwards, Another Scripture, *Writing in a Woman's Voice.*
- Immensity, *Trajectory.*
- The World, *Hibiscus, Poems that Heal and Empower.*
- Makawao Forest, *Muddy River Review.*
- Letter to Franci, *Months to Years.*
- Hidden Places, *Poetry Porch.*
- The Holy Family, Pensive: *A Global Journal of Spirituality and the Arts.*
- A Quiet Language, Evolving Medicine, *The Statement Magazine.*
- The Same and Not The Same, *Riversongs.*
- The Histories We Carry, *Evening Street Review.*
- Present Tension, *The Kerf.*
- The Circle of Life, *Deronda Review*

Published by Human Error Publishing
Paul Richmond
www.humanerrorpublishing.com
paul@humanerrorpublishing.com

Copyright © 2022
by
Human Error Publishing
&
Marguerite Guzmán Bouvard

All Rights Reserved

ISBN: 978-1-948521-72-7

Front Cover:
&
Back Cover
by
Jacques Bouvard

Human Error Publishing asks that no part of this publication be reproduced or transmitted in any form or by any means electronic or mechanical, including photocopy, recording or information storage or retrieval system without permission in writing from Marguerite Guzmán Bouvard and Human Error Publishing . The reasons for this are to help support publisher and the artist.

TABLE OF CONTENTS

Foreword

Present Tension	10
She is Beautiful	11
The Histories We Carry	12
Words	13
Hidden Places	14
Grass Roots	16
Time	17
A Strange Landscape	18
Immensity	20
What Seeds Tell Us	21
Uyghurs	22
Invisible Connections	23
Unraveling	24
Reliving History	25
Two Years Ago	26
Upwards	28
Inner Language	29
Present Tension	30
Upside Down	31
Pollen	32
The Snow Leopard	33
Mundo Verde	34
Unexpected Light	35
Healing	36
Another Scripture	37
Anything Is Possible	39
Our Planet	40
The Trees' Linguistics	41
Light And Shadow	42
George	43
Another Way Of Seeing	45
How Are You	46
A Searing Silence	47
Amy Tan	48
Memory Loss	50

How To Make A Home	51
Evolving Medicine	52
Georgia O'keefe	53
Women's Threads	54
Emaye	55
Praise The Hand	57
A Different Kind Of Music	58
Sophia	59
Cristiana	60
Letter To Franci	61
Paolo	62
Cheryl Softich	63
Another Road	64
Grace	66
Haleakala	67
Silence	68
Uncovering A Palace	69
On Sulphur Mountain	70
Honoring The Hidden Work	71
Vincent Van Gogh	72
Odilon Redon	73
Hope	74
The World	75
Messages	76
Reverend Daniel Alliët	77
The Same And Not The Same	78
The Circle Of Life	79
A Quiet Language	80
Trajectories	81
The Holy Family	82
The Abbey Of Senanque	84
Soaring	85
Forms Of Prayer	86

FOREWORD

Marguerite Guzmán Bouvard latest and last book, Shades of Meaning, wrenches your heart and soothes your soul. Start by reading, "She is Beautiful" and find the inner strength of a mother after "her life was a piece of paper that could be ripped apart."
Read "Cheryl Softich" of bringing suicide awareness to others by honoring her son who was a an Iraq veteran.

In "Present Tension," Bouvard suggests: "May we know more than what / is happening, the trees covered with snow and ice before winter, / folded in on themselves for protection... / that the earth is sacred yet we defile / it. How we must speak to each / other despite the different languages spreading hatred / misunderstanding.
She continues in "Pollen": ... this is the time / of wild flowers we should be / admiring their different colors, / and listening to each other sharing our / stories and our grief, when we need to / learn killing does not solve problems."

In "Healing" for Mary Rosser M.D. espouses healing over confrontation: ... "reminding us that we need to reach out to one another, that caring for / each other is a higher form of healing."
Shades of Meaning cannot say enough about understanding others' losses and compassion for each other. This book unites us like, "Vincent Van Gogh" brings us together by the strong voices / of colors or shapes a solitary painter brings us."

"Hope" is a small incremental process that is fed by light."
While "Messages" are" flickering messages which / are unpredictable, yet always with us / despite our blindness / to the tallest trees and the winds of unseen kindness."

Finally in "Soaring," we soar with Ms. Bouvard's words: "We soar with the words of her journeys, "with their / certainty, just the secret fires that kindle our souls."

As one can see, Marguerite Bouvard's Shades of Meaning communicates lessons on healing and what we have forgotten about being human, like love and caring and deep gratitude for others and ourselves. She continually searches for answers and truths to past oppression and ideology as in the Poem, "Histories We Carry, whereas, " they guide their horses' / bridles with one hand and use / the other to pull apart a man / they arrested by a rope tied / around his hands evoking / a long history of slavery."

With this unforgettable gift, Shades of Meaning injustice is everywhere, yet Ms. Bouvard confronts it head on because she believes, "That we are all in this world to make this world a better place and there are a thousand ways to do so."
How, in her poem, "Hidden Places, her loss is so devastating, it becomes unspeakable: "There is a quiet place inside me / where joy and sorrow are entwined / where I carry the story of another person, / and an understanding comes too late or maybe not seeing the breadth of a life that / has touched yours until that / life has disappeared ."

—Preston H. Hood III, author of "Beauty Is A Cardinal", winner of the 2018, Poet's Seat Poetry Award.

PRESENT TENSION

SHE IS BEAUTIFUL

the woman sitting on a stone
holding her little boy,
with her older child next to her.
She feels that she is nowhere,
in a border between Syria and Iraq,
where the landscape is made of
scattered hay, plastic hanging
over what is supposed to be
a shelter. She is beautiful,
but frightened, anxious, her large
dark eyes holding so much:
the bombing, the destruction
of her home, the town she left behind
along with her language, as if
her life was but a piece
of paper that could be ripped
apart. The word future is now
meaningless. Her face spells
fear, holding a war we turn away
from while we celebrate our withdrawal
from Syria with empty words.

THE HISTORIES WE CARRY

There are actions and images
that carry a wealth of stories,
and that evoke so many
differences. The two men

wearing police uniforms
and cowboy hats in Galveston,
Texas wear the cloaks
of oppression and ideology,

as they guide their horses'
bridles with one hand, and use
the other to pull a black man
they arrested by a rope tied

around his hands, evoking
a long history of slavery.
The man who was mentally ill
and slept outside, was not

a threat. But the president
of the municipal police reacted
by saying, "officers are expected
to follow departmental guidelines."

and they did just that. Limiting
our perspectives, and denial
will always divide us, creating too many
doors that slam inside ourselves.

WORDS

We are so absorbed in our
social media, and insist on
the freedom of expression, even
when hate finds its home there,
like a runaway tiger, where words
are just words even though
they are blood red, and we
celebrate phrases that cause
havoc, shattering the bridges
between us.

HIDDEN PLACES

There is a quiet place inside me,
where joy and sorrow are
intertwined, where I carry
the story of another person,
and understanding comes

too late or maybe not seeing
the breadth of a life that
has touched yours until that
life has disappeared. I think
of all the letters that have

traveled between a black prisoner
and myself, the slow growth
of coming together as friends,
of opening closed doors; the small
one where I had trouble reading

his handwriting, the decision
I made to honor his life with all
its agonies and talents, his reaching
towards the light, his music,
and the sounds of his childhood;

ambulance sirens, shot guns,
car accidents, when he was in a world
that didn't have the maps he
needed to steer a difficult terrain,
the privileges so many of us

take for granted. And then when
the pandemic led to a "lockdown"
of prisons, with the governor of his state
refusing to release the death rate,
his life ended without

notice, I reread a letter that
I failed to treasure, the grace
of a thank you note, of amity,
reaching out and staying
deep inside me, much too late.

GRASS ROOTS

For hope, amity and comprehension
there are the quiet places far
from the newspapers' front pages
and television programs that loudly

tout the latest news which has
been written with perspectives
that are embers and have hidden
layers where people jostle and

disagree. But in a farming town
in Georgia, a blond haired woman
who was willed a farm and a group of
black farmers are having a discussion

on collards and kale. They have
become close friends and work
together over the era of slavery
in a region where white farmers

have confederate flags in their
fields and are proud of their slave
holding ancestors. But these friends
are talking about that history and
how it affected them, working
together in affinity, sharing not only

their thoughts but the loss of one
of their mothers, moving slowly
and quietly through centuries of
obfuscation, cruelty, and pain
with atonement and the quiet
understanding of what love means.

TIME
    for *Valeria Guzmán*

We speak of progress, or of walking towards
changes, but time is also circular, and we find
ourselves in the beginning, in dreams
of wonder, and I am four years old again,
cradling a new doll, a baby with gleaming
black skin whom I rock in my arms
with so much love. I thank my mother
for this gift that would become
an awakening when I was a mother
and a professor, returning to learn
again on my sabbatical so that my students,
who lived within the confines
of their culture, could spread their wings
and read African novels, look more
deeply, remembering that they were
once propelled by wonder,
their souls now finding themselves
in each person they meet.

A STRANGE LANDSCAPE

Who could have foreseen this strange
landscape: empty apartments
with new locks spelling eviction,
a subway with only a few people,
schools without children as if a war

had struck without warning leaving
a new kind of devastation, a tide
not of refugees, but of a new
and complex disease that is moving
throughout our country like a massive

invasion, that knows no boundaries,
the grandmother who lies dying
in the hospital, the man who cannot
breathe, the young woman who
is unable walk because of the pain

in her muscles turns out to be
caused by blood clots. How do
we navigate this new war zone,
with some people driving a bus
because it is essential, some people

working at home, our differences
now magnified, but pain is always
around us like sudden heavy
rain, like wildfires. The soldiers
that are called forth during

this deadly war are doctors, nurses,
emergency technicians who fan
out throughout our country,
like a war zone, yet we are short
of supplies for these soldiers, of supplies

for compassion and understanding
for coming together to face
a pandemic, to move beyond
our differences, arguments, and
denial, to hold each other's hands.

IMMENSITY

Above the Pacific ocean,
massive clouds move slowly
reconfiguring themselves,
carrying rain and light,
but do we ever spend time

looking at immensity or think
about how our planet is in motion,
the Pacific moving on tectonic plates,
and the Hawaiian islands advancing
four inches a year? People on

vacation are reading their iPhones
planning their days, secure under
the umbrellas that protect them
from the burning sun, and do not
notice the extreme increase

in temperature, the rising seas,
the drought that has caused
barren farm fields, the lack
of water for our daily lives,
or the warning that more than

20 million people in Vietnam,
one fourth of its population,
will be inundated by 2050,
and most of Mumbai, India's
financial capital, will be wiped

out. We are living in a cataclysm
that we ignore, when nature
is talking to us, asking us to lift
our eyes and learn how to
reconfigure our lives.

WHAT SEEDS TELL US

The tree tops are filled with what
seems like burgeoning flowers,
but are enclosing seeds that are
scattered by the winds, bringing

forth a wealth that feeds us, and whirls
around us; trees regenerating, the air
vibrating with plenitude-- the way
plants communicate. This is the time

of gifts whose greatest cost
is the need to understand,
to listen and observe, for what takes
care of us in this world needs

to be protected not swept away
as detritus, because we live in
an ecological breakdown, seeing
what is around us as just for

our personal needs, instead
of the mysteries of a never ending
creation where the earth and all
its inhabitants are inseparable.

UYGHURS

A Turkic minority in Xinjiang China
is under intense surveillance, one million
placed in detention camps where
they are forced to learn Mandarin

and criticize their Muslim faith,
yet a woman managed to escape
and flee to Turkey where despite living
in a private apartment she is still

there in her mind with the physical
and sexual abuses gnawing at her.
But she understands that the prisoners
are not statistics, carefully taking

down the names of each woman
who was in her prison cell and putting
them into a notebook, proving
that memories cannot be destroyed,

that there are two realities;
one is endless torture, the other
refusing to make victims invisible,
like the ocean's luminous,

intense blue, cascades of red
and purple flowers in a time of
serious drought, that the light
has its own language.

INVISIBLE CONNECTIONS

Separation is but an illusion;
children who are jumping from
boats, made to catch what lies far below
the water, jump past their short

years that never had room
for laughter or hours when they could
unwind on their own, just so that
we could eat their catch.

Then there are the holidays
with some places wreathed
in light, and some that are no
different. Will we remember how

one life flows into another,
the way rivers and meadows
move together, each at its own
pace, the way the planet's

tectonics flow into each other,
when mountains rise, and plains
unroll, our lives always
changing yet intertwined.

UNRAVELING

The last light on a summer day
is golden and takes a smaller space
on the darkening lawn
or concrete sidewalk, but it is

richer and profound, filled
with memories. While psychologists
claim that toddlers don't have
memories I carry one that has

haunted me and is replicated daily
around the world. I entered life's
mysteries on a large ship crossing
the ocean; the music of my mother's

gentle voice, its kindness enveloping
me, but seeing a long row of people
sitting on the bare deck, backs against
the wall, legs spread out in front

of them, with barely a space between
them, no shelter, and me wondering
why, not knowing that injustice
is part of our lives, that there

will always be refugees, closed doors,
like the ones on our borders,
with hate filled expletives poisoning
the air, the rain pattering against

windows, and there will be corridors
that lead us to unknown places,
unexpected love, the never ending
mysteries of the creation.

RELIVING HISTORY

If you are secretly tracking far right groups
    and their militias,
recording their activities in order to preserve
    a faltering
Democracy, you won't be protected by
    the police. Even
the courts let the prosecuted go free whose
    purpose is violence,
and we will all be Aryans not Jewish,
    Turkish or Syrian,
and can shoot people praying in synagogues
    and mosques
so that Germany will be powerful again
    with the red
calligraphy of blood staining so many
    holy places,
but they cannot kill the story of
    the Turkish father,
fluent in German, who comes to his
    son's grave
and the posters of the murdered everyday
    and stands there
talking quietly about what happened
    with the strength
of rising above unfettered hatred with
    so much dignity.

TWO YEARS AGO

We were in Combloux gazing at
the Alps from our window,
as we have done for so many
years, talking about minor things
as if time had stood still,

but there was a voice inside me
saying, you will not come back
here, and for two years I believed it.
But life is always unpredictable
and after living in the safety

of small perimeters with so much
concern and so many discussions
we packed our bags for the unknown,
and our passage was so very different.
We were wearing masks on the plane,

washing our hands, worried about being
too close to the people around us. And
there were changes when we were
back again: a physician who told us
that she could no longer give vaccines,

because there were death threats
pasted on her office window, angry
voices taking control. And the walks
we loved among glistening meadows,
with the jangle of cow bells, were busy

with crane after crane that demolished
trees, grass, the tender wildflowers
spilling their many colors, a rich
silence that was a world of hope
and never ending growth. But

there are still two worlds:
the physician telling us about
her multilingual daughter who
works for Oxfam in Africa, and
my friend the Haitian cashier

in my town who decided to work
an extra day each week in order to
send money to beleaguered Haiti.
Beneath the rumble of conquest
there are still people reaching

out to help each other; mothers
caring for their children with
so much love, hearts that can never
be silenced, and rays of light
penetrating storm clouds.

UPWARDS

After a heavy and prolonged rain
the flowers whose stalks were
bent on the ground like a waterfall
in stasis, are beginning to slowly

rise up, at a time when we all
need to move upward from what
assails us. The trees are making new
shoots, people are reaching out

to each other in small ways;
the quiet ongoing process in Israel
with Sheikh Raed Bader and
Rabbi Michael Melchior working

together for peace in a country
where religions and nationalities
are raging against each other,
showing us that our Creator

does not have only one name,
that we need to honor every
life over the distinctions
that separate us when the colors

of the sunset with its intertwining
clouds bring together the sea,
earth and sky, the light that ushers
each one of us to life.

INNER LANGUAGE

There was an ant in our hallway
that I stepped on when
my granddaughter cried out,
that it was carrying a crumb,
her vision wider and deeper
reminding me that life
is burgeoning everywhere
with the mothers of all creatures
preparing meals for their
offspring, that we are
all interconnected, relying
on each other in so many different
ways, reading the language
of gestures, movement and
expressions, the way she rests
on her bed after a long day's
work with an arm enfolding
her cat, the warmth of its
presence in her quiet studio

PRESENT TENSION

May we know more than what
is happening, the trees covered
with snow and ice before winter,
folded in on themselves for protection

with some branches torn off,
that the land is telling us something,
we are fragile, and predictability
was never with us, that we should

learn what was always there
waiting for us, how inside of us
there are always discoveries
we turn away from,

that the earth is sacred, but we defile
it, how we must speak to each
other despite the different
languages spreading hatred

and misunderstanding, that we
must cooperate on our brief
journey for all our children
and our children's offspring,

although there are different
countries, regions and counties,
they all need to restore the balance
of thriving trees, the angle of geese

the hand reaching out to restore,
to create links that bind us together,
and even to remember what we
have lost -- the word together.

UPSIDE DOWN

Did he ever stop to think,
the truck diver who roared
up the curb to crash into
a group of Asian Americans

having a picnic in a park,
threatening them by brandishing
a knife, causing them
to flee, than stay at home,

afraid of even walking outside --
driven by words poisoned
by hatred, his mind shut down,
his feelings a wildfire

spinning out of control, blinded
to what connects us.

POLLEN

In late May what swirls around us
in unprecedented numbers is pollen
flying through the air, the signs

of new life, and new beginnings
in a time when the Israelis
and Palestinians are killing each

other during a celebration at the end
of Ramadan in a mosque, or in a settlement,
and in neighborhoods where they once

lived together, and can no longer
do so, when they have lost their
way, and the meaning of the words

that guide us through our lives.
Pollen can fit in our hands yet contains
a universe of happenings: the male

microgamelophytes produce sperm cells
to female reproductive pistils. When placed
on a stigma of a flowering plant

a pollen grain creates a tube which grows
down the tissue to the ovary, a familiar
pairing which is about families

that bond without borders. This is the time
of wildflowers when we should be
admiring their different colors,

and listening to each other, sharing our
stories and our grief, when we need to
learn that killing does not solve problems.

THE SNOW LEOPARD

is an elusive and graceful presence
hidden among the high rugged slopes,
veiled during heavy snowfalls
in isolated areas in Pakistan, a predator
inspiring interest around the world,

especially in the West. A group
of photographers journeyed there to film
it for a television program, spending
months tracking it down. Nissa Mallek,
a Pakistani journalist joined them,

with a more complex view of the snow
leopard whom he regards as an
ambassador. He disagreed with a scientist
who put a collar on the leopard in order to use
telemetry that would transmit its location

by satellite, and thus save it. Nissa Mallek
found it disrespectful, or we can live
with nature in other ways. He showed the photos
to a group of school children whose parents
were concerned because they lived close to it

with a growing population. They all shouted
with joy, seeing it as a friend not an enemy.
For Nissa Mallek, the leopard is a legend,
a mystical creature that touches him deeply, finding
it distressing to tame nature that is sacred.

MUNDO VERDE

There are walls that are built
to counter the rising seas
with concrete lining the streets

and highways, but there are
also the protective arms
of the mangroves with their roots

in the sea water, their branches
linked so closely that it is difficult
to penetrate them. They are

guardians that watch over the fisheries
people rely on in places like
Rincon de Mar, Colombia,

safeguarding us from strong winds,
telling us how water, sky,
and earth communicate,

what the aborigines have
known for millennia, that
we must respond to them with

our whole beings like the Maori
who have been always intent
on fulfilling their stewardship.

UNEXPECTED LIGHT

It could have been a far off
galaxy because I had never seen

this play of light before, –
at midnight, while all the windows

were dark, the shadows of trees
and branches were splayed against

the luminescent layers
of snow piled high before the circle

of houses, and on the streets,
as if the light that suffused the air

was emanating from the snow,
as well as the moon,

telling me that this unexpected
illumination has its own story.

HEALING
for Mary Rosser, M.D.

Reading the news about the number of people
infected with Covid-19, the rising curve
of deaths among the people who
were the most vulnerable: minorities

who did the essential work, and their zip codes,
immigrants living in apartments so crowded
they rented their beds while they worked
their night shifts. And in this country

which is already so divided, some of us
have put our hearts and minds on hold
because they have higher needs; businesses
shut down, restaurants, stores, and bars

needing to open, some marching for freedom
with their rifles. But then there are the nurses
and physicians, working around the clock,
holding their patients' hands, putting

their own lives at risk, joining our
grieving, reminding us that we need to reach
out to one another, that caring for
each other is a higher form of healing.

ANOTHER SCRIPTURE

There is the calligraphy of shadows
that scroll across the skin of gleaming
snow, and on tree barks,

with the earth continually rewriting
its holy book, a quiet way
of entering our lives

that encompasses every country,
every map we want to rewrite, telling us
how every moment is filled

with so much meaning, that we need
to pause, and change our pace,
so that a moment can become

an ocean that holds us
in its arms, a meadow with
its fields of burgeoning flowers,

so we can discover that
we need to care for each other,
like our Asian Americans

we have mistreated for decades
creating so many new
borders they cannot cross,

so we can untangle presence
and absence in our daily
lives, and in our perspectives.

If we take a moment to open
the windows of our hearts
and let the spirit guide us,

we will see more deeply
and gain an understanding,
awakening us to a wider world.

ANYTHING IS POSSIBLE
for Edwin Soto

Take the sky, one moment rays
of light rest on the balcony, the continent
of clouds opens to reveal a deep blue,
then the wind's absence, yet the air

exudes humidity, the possibility of rain,
just like the unexpected decisions that shape
our lives by a group of men huddled
together in a palace proclaiming

that the frequent loss of land the size
of a football field by rising sea levels
is of no consequence, like the drought
and high heat that invade our forests

causing unexpected fires. But a young teenager
in a poor neighborhood is writing poems
about police patrolling the streets, and the fear
that pervades them, yet his verses

are the wildflowers that greet us during
our arduous journeys, like the sudden smile
of a person you pass by that opens up a place
inside yourself, a little child laughing.

OUR PLANET

I looked out of the window and the sky
was cerulean blue, the white clouds
soaring at their own pace, transforming
themselves, carrying gentle shadows,
the slope was a tender green flecked
with the rusting of Autumn, just a page
of our planet that is caving in with
relentless heat, raging fires, heavy rain
and the anarchy of a new generation.
But the endings have their own stories;
rivers of blood and anger while the earth
keeps turning the pages of its book
with the trees, clouds, the birth of seeds
cracking the hardened soil, while we
believe in our finite descriptions of time.

THE TREES' LINGUISTICS

What we lose in our quickening pace
in this world is the ability to
see and to reflect. When my computer
turned itself off on my desk,
I saw a stunning and unexpected
view of the maple tree just outside
my window on its empty screen,
drawing me towards it in a new
way as if it were speaking
to me in its quiet majesty, its own
harmonics, no longer carrying the sun's
trajectory, but it's own stillness
and profundity, its inner language,
so that we who are continually
focused on our cell phones and social
media have forgotten to think about
time in a different way: the weather
of events around the world and
how they have impacted so many
people in different ways, our own
history, and what is occurring
in our crowded cities. If we slow down
to reflect we will move through centuries
like the trees, we will keep learning
about our many connections,
the complexities and the often
hidden beauty of our lives.

LIGHT AND SHADOW

GEORGE

        You showed up unexpectedly
at my high school graduation with a car salesman
        you met along the way.
It seems as if you always preferred strangers
        exchanging a few words
then moving away on your own route
        unencumbered.

I was 13 when I came to stay with you in Mexico
        where a young French woman
who was to be my companion introduced me
        to a man her own age whom
she called her uncle, where you told me
        not to speak English
as I listened to you and your colleagues in bars
        while I doodled on paper.

Evenings you took me to nightclubs with them
        and ordered me whiskey sours.
I never knew what your job was, or who
        you really were.
You could have been a stranger, but then you were
        charming to strangers.

When I was 17, I came to stay in your Sao Paulo
        apartment with its balcony
where you sat puffing on your cigar.
        Evenings, we walked
along Rua Andrade. and you stopped
to speak to a man dragging an empty box,
        went to the Rotary Club
where you introduced me as the child who had
        no other parent but you.

You took me to nightclubs with your friends
        where I watched topless dancers,
but I was never to go out alone with a person
        of the opposite sex.

You drove me to the port of Santos where you
        strode up to a policeman
and asked him where the black market was then
        bought me a carton of cigarettes,
a gift I never asked for from a person who didn't
        know who I was.

Far from the world of my mother and grandmother
        of affection and good manners,
of consistency and predictability, I watched you
        speak so many languages
and learned them myself, for you did teach me
        something -- but not the one
that you never spoke, the exotic words of courtesy,
        commitment and love.

ANOTHER WAY OF SEEING
for Ariel

Looking back in time is not what
it seems. Take a 15 month old
baby-girl who is deep in thought,

trying to open a closed window
with its metal handle, for opening
is a way of traveling through

time, is a scenario of so many
episodes, and an array of different
paths she discovered, who

is so dexterous as she picks
up a colored pencil, assesses it,
then makes a blank page come

alive, something that decades
later will be a powerful portrait
speaking to our inner selves.

Then slide back to a three-year-old
lying on the floor and playing
dominoes quietly, the minutes

passing as if there were none.
Traveling through time
is not just to see the smiles

and sweetness of a young child
but is about a journey
of becoming, about self-made

paths, a light that blazes
through joyous and
difficult times.

HOW ARE YOU
for Mirlande Butler

a short query thousands
of times, wanting the one word
that obliterates the richness
of our lives: when the sky

shimmered, when it darkened,
how events that were never
replicated were like buds opening,
the smile of a granddaughter

that holds a world in itself,
then the silence between
two friends that is suddenly
opened like a window,

her thoughts about a close
friend who has slipped out
of her days, a door has closed,
"how can it be, the work

she did for so many people
stilled, her children, the path
she defined, how can it be?"
There are silences to be

shared, pools of light accepting
the shadows of our lives.

A SEARING SILENCE
for Jean-Claude Gallez

There are many kinds of silences:
    the one of reverence
before prayers, the one during a solitary
    walk when your vision
is focused on the road before you, and your
    thoughts are forming
into intentions, night time when the traffic
    of nearby highways
and our daily lives has stopped, but there is
    one that is neither
a precursor nor cyclical like our nights and days --
    causing a storm in
your heart that no one hears -- your son who
    was part of your life,
whom you watched grow into a man with his
    children gathering
around him, and you, wanting to tell him
    so many things who
has slipped out of time into a searing silence.

AMY TAN

Because your mother kept trying
        to commit suicide,
opening the car door when it was
        moving, and you
were in the back seat, frightened,
        feeling so alone,
because she also had a moment
        of violence that
frightened you, and chided you
        as you were growing
up, but you did mature into a loving
        marriage, using your
pen to move toward understanding,
        and flew to Shanghai
with her, meeting your unknown
        brothers and sisters,
learned why she had run away
        with your father
and you began to talk to her while
        she poured out
her history, bit by bit, that she was
        a concubine
in a terrible marriage, the word love
        erased everyday,
not only for herself but for her small
        boy who was ill yet
whose father didn't care, all those lost
        years pouring out
because you opened her up, and listened
        to her hidden grief
that was also a severe case of
        PTSD. You saved
her by listening, not realizing
        that it was healing,
so that before she died, she spoke
        two words to you
for the first time, that she loved
        you, and was sorry

for all she did to you over the years,
      yet you still carry
the past with you, and its sorrows,
      learning that what
lies within so many of us shouldn't
      be hidden or ignored.

MEMORY LOSS

There was a woman
who struggled with her
memory, with words
and phrases, what so many

people take for granted,
her friends, the people she
would see in many places,
perfect strangers. She found

that the roads we take from
our inner selves, translating
her thoughts, feelings and
insights have changed

as if she were lost on an
island in the middle
of a large ocean, or sent
to a country with a different

and difficult language
for just a few days, and no
time to learn. We all need
wings to carry us through

our days, work, nights, travel,
and celebrations, the music
of translating what lies
in the depths of our hearts.

HOW TO MAKE A HOME

Hang a print by Maillol on the wall,
trees with intertwined branches
and their many stories of time
and weather, a flower pot with

a rose and tiny purple blooms,
a lamp to guide us through
dark times, a drawer with needle
and threads to repair our

broken days, a sturdy table
where we share our thoughts
and events, coming together,
a shelf filled with books

that will guide us in so many
ways, the windows that
bring in rivers of air
with their ever changing

tides, heavy rain, gentle
rain, the quiet whispering
of snow, a door that we can
open where we are able

to sleep, dream, a familiar
setting where we are known
and can hold our days,
our nights, time that is

so fragile also bringing
us to unknown paths.

EVOLVING MEDICINE

How to move past pain. See the good things
around you. Early after a sleepless night
you look out of the window
when the darkness is beginning
to fade. You look up and see a broad
tree trunk standing guard, a cloud
of green leaves far above the houses,
the tall trunks, you see the marvelous,
the sky speaking to you.

And this no matter what is a way
of continuing, despite physicians
who are so busy that they feel
overwhelmed, and when I talk to them
through their aides, nurses, the world
of in betweens, it's as if I were speaking
a foreign language. When your body
hurts, when your injured brain is slowing
down your path, the spirit that
wants to fly is now jumping through
hoops, unable to penetrate the buzz
and fog of all the in betweens.

Then I stand up, to enter the day
when I see an evergreen
silent in its plenitude, how understanding
needs no words, and how compassion
only takes place between equals
like the nurse who works with
dying Covid-19 patients, and tells me,
"I am one of them."

GEORGIA O'KEEFE

We tend to think of flowers as
small decorations, what we
welcome on special occasions,
but for Georgia O'Keefe
they are many pulpits:
a line of shimmering light
in enormous black robes,
dark purple and black
flames rising among clouds
of many hued greens. Her
flowers are in slow graceful
motion, embracing the sky,
sending us their own
messages about the never
ending creation, about
beauty and grace.

WOMEN'S THREADS

My mother laying out patterns
for the beautiful dresses she designs,
but also calculating dimensions, speaking

the language of mathematics as well as
the one of visual art, while I plunged
into the world of political science

in front of the classroom then wrote
the language of clouds interspersed
with light, the poetry that spirals

out of what whirls around me, and
in far off countries, my daughter
whose singular voice makes so many

different characters come alive, also
speaks so many languages,
Farsi, Italian, French, who loves

collecting their special music, plus
the language of computers, my granddaughter
whose drawings bring courageous

faces that speak from the wall,
as well as the grace of flowers blooming,
is adept at analyzing digital data,

our geography spanning from
so many different continents.
But what binds us travels beyond

time -- women sewing, drawing,
and reflecting, gathering the threads
that hold the world together.

EMAYE

For people who don't know
what that word means
and who still believe that
families are only biological,
they can learn that it means

Wonderful Mother, that
Abebech Gobena, returning
from a pilgrimage to
a holy site in Addis Ababa,
only to see people dying

of famine at the road side
with a baby trying to suckle
at her dead mother's breast,
gently picked her up,
wrapped her in a cloth

and brought her home, returning
the next day to give these
people bread and water,
taking more children home
until she had 21 living with her.

When her husband refused
to take in any more, she left him
to live in a shack in the woods,
and cooked for an income
not only to support them but also

to pay a tutor to educate her
children. As she kept taking
in more and more, she created
a non-profit orphanage, bought
farmland outside of the city

with free school for hundreds
of children, HIV/AIDS prevention.
and helped them succeed in life.
When she died at 85 of Covid-19,
a former orphan wrote, After

getting my diploma I started
working with her, "She was
a mother above mothers,
with an open heart that knows
no limits, an Emaye."

PRAISE THE HAND

that guides needle
and thread, that ushers
clay into eloquence.
Praise the hand that patiently
repairs what is broken,
the hand that coaxes music
out of metal scrap.
Praise the hand in the hand
that moves beyond
the brevity of flesh.

A DIFFERENT KIND OF MUSIC

In Maui, a tree was listening
to the music of the wind, bent
to its rhythms, as its longest

branch curved over the harp
of the ocean, again and
again, until the notes were

written on the sky's open
pages. This is how the deepest
music is written that transforms

us: meeting your lover for
the first time when he was walking
behind you on the sidewalk,

commenting on your legs
in a language you were not
supposed to understand, that

turned into a new world where
like trees we hold memories
in our tangled roots, the music

of our offspring's voices,
the murmuring of wings,
leaves and heartbeats.

SOPHIA

It must have been the sun
that gilded your curls, that opened
your smile like a flower and sent its rays
spinning through your laughter.
It must have been the sky
that took refuge in your eyes,
their weather now grave and pensive
now joyous as a summer afternoon
in Provence. It must have been a memory
from before you were even a thought
that lives in your tiny hands
as they carefully fit one shape
into another with precision.
It must have been written somewhere
that your secret kingdom
will one day bear sheltering groves.

CRISTIANA

A moment of peace, the dove's syllable
above the chatter of sparrows, blue jays,

and cardinals, reminding us
to listen, a moment when the leaves

from the tallest branches blaze just before
sundown, after a long winter,

with its unpredictable gales. My cousin
Maria Teresa's daughter in the harsh white

of a hospital In Brescia – a flame held
in the circle of her parents, her lanky son,

blossoming daughter – suddenly quenched.
And a swirl of light rising upwards

towards the sky, this life we so cherish,
all our yesterdays, a brief moment.

LETTER TO FRANCI

Suddenly the world has changed and the sound
      of your mother's voice is gone.
Suddenly people remark how mature you have
      become, but you are still only
a child. At a family dinner surrounded by cousins
      who have parents and siblings
you are praised for your beautiful new dress
      with its white pleats and dark top,
but you carry an absence that no one sees, the wounds
      that strike us all with their own
language and that lives in our hearts. Your mother
      should be sitting in the audience
at your dance recital, listening to your stories
      with the understanding that
entwined you. But you will always carry her ways
      that will become part of you,
the way she saw life in a flower rising from the earth,
      in a blade of grass, with the wisdom
of the Native Americans, the summoning of love,
      the invisible glow of her being.

PAOLO

There was a family dinner in my cousin's house
in Sistiana, six months after Cristiana's

funeral, when we all came together from different
parts of the world, and when the table

was vibrant with our conversations, but there was a
man at the end of the one side

of the table who never said a word. When I looked
at him puzzled, Cristiana's father

introduced me, this is Paolo, he and Cristiana
were planning to grow old together,

he was with her every moment, making her laugh,
even at the end,

and Paolo replied, "every moment has its own eternity,"
like the clouds flaming above

darkened fields, the flamboyant hibiscus
whose petals open for only

a day, like the love blazing in our hearts
that cannot be extinguished.

CHERYL SOFTICH

When her son committed
suicide because of the PTSD
that overtook him after his
return from Iraq, his mother

began what turned into years
of work to preserve his
memory, fired by a profound
love of her son Noah, anger

that he received no care for his
trauma, that too many people
were not concerned about
his death. She contacted members

of Congress, local officials
determined that her son would
not be regarded as a statistic,
but as a hero, who gave his life

for his country, dedicating herself
to his memory, contacting Bridges
For The Fallen only to be told
that it was for soldiers who were

killed in action. In response she
spent five years trying to get
a law passed that would include
soldiers who died of PTSD.

On August, 21, 2021 on
PTSD Awareness Day, a sign
was unveiled on a bridge
with his name Specialist

Noah Pierce, celebrating how
he made a difference in
our country, and that the real
power in this world is love.

ANOTHER ROAD

A tree is bruised just above
ground, a large wound
like flesh that has been
torn by an onslaught.
Yet its branches are
sturdy, reaching out
in every direction and
across a path, filled
with dark green leaves
that cool us with their
shadows, as well as
lighting our way, teaching
us that growth is not
a straight journey,
and that we learn in
so many different ways
that bring us to more
profound perspectives.

GRACE

HALEAKALA

At Haleakala we move with the slow
rhythm of the rising clouds,

the pulse of motion where the sky
and earth are one, in an immensity

where we are smaller than
the miniature wildflowers that deck

the road with their blazing colors,
we who are always enmeshed

in our daily lives of work, family
and home. But the ancient Hawaiians

revered the volcano where they lived
and understood its complexities,

the Ohelo that grows on cooled lava,
with its generous fruits, and is

sacred to the goddess Pele, who warned them
of eruptions, the Ahinahina (silversword)

whose silver blades deflect the sun
and store water. Worship was part

of their everyday lives as they honored
the sacredness of the creation.

SILENCE

brings us the radiance of that vast
invisible world that is pulsating
within us and around us,

the many dimensions
of being, the understanding
that the true and boundless power

is love. We need silence and solitude
for our souls to flourish, to move past
the noise, the chatter, the desire

to be more important than another
person. As we walk through
life's journey, humility opens the doors

that separate us from the marginalized
and the misunderstood, helping us to see
the beauty within them, to know

that we are all connected to every living being,
flowers, bees, a bird's wing,
to know that we are in the hospital

with a child who has been wounded
in a war, that we are made of light,
not only of flesh and bone.

UNCOVERING A PALACE

In Cancún a Mayan palace
is buried beneath layers of jungle
yet still throbbing with mute
voices; jade, obsidian, pyrite,
and eloquent stone fretwork,
but no shrines for the gods,
no weapons for warfare,
just angels of sap and earth.

ON SULPHUR MOUNTAIN

A friend asked me to visit the library,
to consult the tomes about myths
and religion, but instead I took a gondola

to Sulphur Mountain and stood
in the clear air where the peaks glittered
like an ocean's stilled waves, and a raven

dipped and soared like a soul
released. The silence hummed, drowning
out the gaggle of tourists

with their cameras and binoculars.
Such visions journey within our dreams
like the cup of water that gives us

life, the sacred stick blossoming
into nations, the man breaking his chains
inside Plato's cave of shadows,

like the bread and wine
we lift beneath the solar flame
in the vast chambers of ourselves.

HONORING THE HIDDEN WORK

Praise the spider's work
of weaving, the monarch butterflies
criss-crossing the frigid air
over continents, and the rock worm
laying foundations for the cathedrals
of coral reefs. Praise the loom
that is never stilled
the persistence
and strength of fragility.

VINCENT VAN GOGH

There are many kinds of currents
not just in the eddies of water,
but in Vincent Van Gogh's
paintings where the corners

of the world come alive;
the undulating mountains,
the swirl of grass, tree bark,
and branches, the cloudy sky

where the fishing boats
on the beach in Camargue
are not stilled. Everything is
pulsating with its own

rhythm, like the ones that
are hidden, such as tree
roots that intertwine with
fungus, and the mycelium

of mushrooms, and that what
is multilayered beneath
the soil, is also the different
meanings we see in our daily

lives which are revealed
by the strong voices
of colors and shapes
a solitary painter brings us.

ODILON REDON*

Do we ever look at the sky
the way we gaze at the ocean
with its beauty, majesty and
tumult? But for Odilon Redon,

the sky is an ocean blazing
with intense colors, peopled
with the profile of a woman
surrounded by halos of gold-green

light, with a swath of white
across her chest, and what could
be a comet blazing across her
makes the stars seem like pinpoints

and the earth with its miniature
cathedral is bathed in a circle
of tiny stars. And there are
arrays of horses galloping

against the clouds that are
suffused with different colors,
some of them borne by wings.
We all see butterflies around

us, but not the size of horses,
a myriad of rich colors, flying
in different directions and
speeds. For Odilon Redon

the sky is where the mysteries
of our lives and spirits are
palpable, transforming
our visions and beliefs.

_____

*French painter, 1840-1916.

HOPE

Living day by day, slowly we unwind
the time that seems stilled
with the darkness of Covid-19
inside a dwelling that harbors

both isolation, memories
of places we went, the loved ones
we cannot visit, and the thoughts
of all who have lost their

family members -- a months old
poinsettia has sprouted
miniature buds, with tiny
leaves, the new colors of pale green

and crimson reminding us
of how far we have come,
a small incremental process
that is fed by light.

THE WORLD

The ocean with its dark currents
could hold us in
its power, yet the world kneels
everywhere, a shell
washed up with its glowing
colors, fragile, is reborn
because beauty can never
be extinguished.

MESSAGES

Light moves like water, rushing
in whorls, flickering
messages from the wind,
the tallest trees, which is
unpredictable yet
always with us

like the man who crosses
the border into Mexico
with food and dignity
bags for the undocumented
immigrants, with the humble
gifts of soap and tooth brushes,
a love of the marginalized
and mistreated,

flickering messages which
are unpredictable yet
always with us
despite our blindness
to the tallest trees
and the winds of
unseen kindness.

REVEREND DANIEL ALLIĚT

a retired Catholic priest presides
over a church in Brussels
that has no pews, no votive candles,
nor worshippers, and the statues

of saints are draped with
posters on social justice. The marble
floor is crowded with mattresses
and sleeping bags for undocumented

immigrants. For him, the core
of Christianity is helping
the marginalized, and he has devoted
his life to them who are also

his housemates from Morocco, Rwanda,
Guinea, and Senegal. He has
offended the more conservative
bishops that wanted to turn

the church into a museum, and
also populist politicians,
creating a singular path which
reflects a different view

of reality, that we are all
one, and that in his words,
"God is too great to lock him
up in one religion."

THE SAME AND NOT THE SAME

Everything is different, but the same,
the trees we tended over
the years are now soaring
like steeples: maples, lindens, the white

pines, another world that has
its own voices, like the wind
that has changed as it keeps forming
its own trajectory, and has

so many stories. There are languages
all around us that speak of the fire
of becoming, the swirling leaves
telling us that the earth and sky

encompass us, that it vibrates
inside us awakening us to its
splendors, and the fierce pattern
of survival, that everything

changes; heavy branches tumble,
sand becomes silent rocks,
oceans rise and fall but there
is always a beginning.

THE CIRCLE OF LIFE

Pin oaks, lindens and maple trees
are stripped bare, their limbs
seem to be touching the sky,
their naked strength and beauty,

their branches stretching out
as if they were lifting a weight
we cannot fathom, with so much
grace, and a deeper kind of knowing,

and in the distance, the pin oak
is holding just a few last leaves,
its gleaming gems. The air is filled
with cascades of falling leaves

that are liberated as if they were
unwrapping themselves from
flesh and bone, flying is so many
different directions, and my long

gone Cherokee friend, Awiakta,
is still singing in the seeds,
the many dimensions of being,
the turning of time.

A QUIET LANGUAGE

We are not alone in this
shifting world, but are gifted
with abundance, with leaves piled up
on the cool ground of Autumn,
while some remain up high
the color of burnt gold. We are not
alone as the sunlight pierces
the tallest trees because everything
is alive and breathing, squirrels
bouncing across the branches,
chipmunks dashing across the roads
at top speed, but we fill our ears
with new music blasting from
passing cars, as if time were
spinning, forgetting that silence
has so many different voices,
that if we open the doors
of memory, and all that lives
in our hearts we will find abundance,
that our separation from each
other, from the precious land that
is so much older and wiser than
we are is but an illusion.

TRAJECTORIES

In Autumn, the early morning light
comes from the highest tree tops
moving very slowly in gradients
so that the darkness is transformed

and we are looking at the world
that is so hungry for hope:
the refugees crossing the ocean
in crowded unsafe boats, the immigrants

we turn away at our borders because
the walls we build are in our hearts.
But if we take the time to watch the slow
diffusion of light: the Baptist minister

sending money to Haitian immigrants
so that they can reach safety in his
community, our black people in
Tennessee and North Carolina,

who have suffered so much in our
medical institutions, deciding to take
vaccinations, a world renowned
novelist refusing a translation

of her latest work in Israel because
of their treatment of the Palestinians,
we will slowly and quietly reach
luminescence, the path towards mutuality.

THE HOLY FAMILY

The Messiah is supposed to have
only one meaning, but one
can be many when there is
an illumination in a dark corner
of the world, and Messiah
is not age related, like the seven

year old Messiah and his
older sister Reign which does
not mean queen, but giving
everything she has, to love
and protect. When he was only
four years old and was unable

to walk because of a rare disease,
she played with him, took tender
care of him, and never left
his side. Nor is the Messiah
white as the Western world
portrays him, but the color

of the night sky, with the radiant
stars of his parents Toka
who spoke of blessings when
Reign gave him her bone marrow
for a transplant, and Will who
would visit his hospital room

and sing to him. At home Toka
sang "This is the day the Lord made",
and they both gave graciously
from the little they had;
an envelope of money when
a friend lost his job, Burger King

coupons when another person
was laid off, bags of clothes,
for giving was their joy.
But just when Messiah began
to be able to walk, he showed
symptoms of the coronavirus

and died in his hospital bed.
But Messiah and Reign
remain intertwined because
though they were only a few years
on this earth they understood
the meaning of eternity.

THE ABBEY OF SENANQUE

was built in 1148 in the valley
beneath Gordes in the South of France
for monks who wanted to spend their life
in prayer and contemplation. It is made
of eloquent stone with arches upon
arches at different levels so that even
the high windows are arches, just
stone, no embellishments to distract us
in our search for grace, and is a place
where we enter the mystery of
the creation, where the past, present
and future are intertwined, and we enter
ourselves, finding an immensity
to ponder in our brief time on this earth.

SOARING

The prayers and meditation
that lift you out of a room
into an unimagined spaciousness
as if you had wings that
take you on a journey, is a way
into a mystery, a love so powerful
it has no words, leaving all
that you have learned, the wonder
of a passage not written in hymns
or beneath the temples and spires
that shelter us with their
certainty, just the secret fires
that kindle our souls.

FORMS OF PRAYER

1
A longing that issues
from a cello,
annihilating time.

2
Befriending a stranger,
speaking with
an enemy.

3
Bearing the weight
of our endurance
with quiet grace.

4
Planting olive trees
in the chambers
of the heart.
Tilling fields
for the next generation.

ABOUT THE AUTHOR

Marguerite Guzmán Bouvard's poetry books have won two awards, the Quarterly Review of Literature award and the MassBook Award for Poetry. She has received awards for her poems from Blue Mesa Press, and the Moon prize from Writing in a Woman's Voice. She is a former professor of Political Science and Poetry as well as giving lectures on climate change. She has also written a number of non-fiction books on Social Justice, Human Rights, Grief, Illness and The Invisible Wounds of War. Her book, Revolutionizing Motherhood: the Mothers of the Plaza de Mayo, has been cited around the world in Croatia, Denmark, Austria, Poland, France, Switzerland, Israel, Sweden, Romania, Indonesia, Israel, Spain, Ecuador, Brazil, Argentina, and Iran.

www.ingramcontent.com/pod-product-compliance
Lightning Source LLC
Chambersburg PA
CBHW031207090426
42736CB00009B/810